THIS BOOK BELONGS TO:

....

....

BY MOOREA SEAL

JOURNALS

The 52 Lists Project

52 Lists for Happiness

52 Lists for Togetherness

52 Lists for Calm

STATIONERY

52 Lists Planner

52 Lists Postcards

52 Lists "My Weekly List" Desk Pad

52 Lists "To Do List" Notepad

BOOKS

Make Yourself at Home

52 Lists
for
Calm

JOURNALING INSPIRATION
for SOOTHING ANXIETY *and*
CREATING A PEACEFUL LIFE

BY MOOREA SEAL

SASQUATCH BOOKS
SEATTLE

To my therapist. It is my dream to make sure everyone has the opportunity to be guided and inspired by someone like you, be it within the realm of counseling or simply in everyday life. You are the person who has encouraged and empowered me to research, study, and apply all I have learned about mental health and anxiety management to my own life, and in turn, I have the privilege of sharing that through this journal with so many others. If just one person is inspired by my letter to you and gains the courage to find their own therapist, I will feel fulfilled. It only takes one person to make a difference in someone's life, and you have been that person who helped me find calm and true relief amidst anxiety. Thank you for all that you do and all that you are.

I t's perfectly normal to experience stress and anxiety. Just like happiness and anger have their reasons for existing within us, anxiety serves an important purpose as well. *Anxiety* has been defined as "a feeling of worry, nervousness, or unease, typically about an imminent event or something with an uncertain outcome." Our body creates that anxious sensation (which can manifest physically, cerebrally, and/or emotionally) for a purpose: to aid us in being aware of ourselves and our surroundings. But there are times when anxiety and stress can get out of hand, when our body and mind go on high alert when it would serve us better to experience calm.

Everyday stress that is manageable is different from a medically diagnosed anxiety disorder. According to the Anxiety and Depression Association of America, forty million adults in the United States, age eighteen and older, live with an anxiety disorder, and I am one of them. I was diagnosed with anxiety in my early twenties, alongside depression. And what was misdiagnosed in my childhood as attention deficit disorder, or ADD, was later rediagnosed as complex post-traumatic stress disorder, or C-PTSD.

There is no one reason that anyone develops an anxiety disorder. For me, it was probably a combination of many things: learned behavior from my family (many of whom live with anxiety and depression); an innate tendency to ruminate and overthink; a propensity for being very sensitive, intuitive, and empathic; the impact of traumatic experiences in my past; chemical imbalances in my body; allergies, inflammation, and gut issues—the list goes on. As you can see, it's pretty tricky nailing down exactly why anxiety disorders happen, but with help, relief is possible.

This journal is not an anxiety-diagnosing tool. But what this journal does provide is a space for you to find calm in the everyday, so that you can manage stress and anxiety with more ease. You'll get a chance to develop that positive and affirming voice within you: your intuition—that deep-down subliminal processing of information too complex for rational thought, which can help you move through difficult situations with more clarity. You will learn to take the time to ground yourself in the present, so that you can get to know your inner world on a deeper level. You'll get a chance to release your thoughts and feelings as you create your lists and try the guided exercises that go along with them. Each of them is specially designed to help you gain a new way to cope with and relieve stress, so that each day will become a little calmer.

Before you start this journey, take a moment to acknowledge your intuition. Visualize your intuition within you as a little flickering light, a child, your younger self, or a comforting animal. Perhaps the stress and anxiety within you is your intuition saying, "Hey! I need some help here!" That intuition deserves your attention, so that together you can create the calm you desire. Close your eyes. Tell that little light, "I trust you. I see you. I am here for you. I embrace you. You are here within me for a reason. And together, we will grow, we will heal, and we will create a calmer life as I trust in you and you trust in me."

LET THE JOURNEY TO CALM BEGIN.

Xo Moorea Seal

Get Together

You've picked up this book; you're reading this page. You are present in the here and now, and you're curious as to how you can make today and tomorrow a little bit better by cultivating calm in your life. And so many others are on this journey with you throughout the world!

Use the hashtag **#52ListsforCalm** when posting about your lists on social media, and explore the 52 Lists community's posts to see the insights others are gathering from their list making! What you share online or on social media about your lists may help and inspire others in their journeys toward calm as well. And with each of our efforts in helping ourselves, we are cultivating a more peaceful world, from the world within you to the world around you.

Learn more about the 52 Lists series at
MooreaSeal.com/pages/52Lists.

Other hashtags to explore:
#52ListsProject | #52Lists | #52HappyLists
#52ListsforHappiness | #52ListsforTogetherness

Contents

Be Present

Look Back

Move Forward

Release

The secret of health for both mind and body is not to mourn for the past, nor to worry about the future, but to live the present moment wisely and earnestly.

—GAUTAMA BUDDHA

———————

Modern society encourages us to strive for the future from the moment we are conscious. We plan and set expectations for our future selves and for those we love, with hopes for something bigger and better. But what if we were to give ourselves permission to focus on the present? It's a beautiful thing to strive for betterment for yourself and the world around you, but just as importantly, you deserve acceptance and peace right now, in the physical space you are in, in the body you are in, in your present thoughts and feelings, and amidst whatever stresses may be weighing on you.

Being present in the here and now is possible. And the present is where we must continually exist to cultivate true inner calm. In a world that rewards perfection and pushing ourselves beyond our limits, it is the greatest act of rebellion to believe that who and where you are *right now* is exactly who and where you need to be.

———————

YOU ARE CAPABLE.

List 1

LIST EVERYTHING YOU ARE
THINKING ABOUT *RIGHT NOW*.

....

....

....

....

....

....

....

....

....

....

....

....

....

....

....

....

....

....

....

....

....

....

CLARIFYING EXERCISE: Cross out all of the things on your list that you *cannot* do right in this moment. Circle only one thing that you actually want to do right now, or a thought that feels helpful and positive. Go do your one thing, or just hold that helpful thought with you throughout the day.

List 2

TAKE ONE MINUTE TO FOCUS AND CHECK IN WITH EACH OF YOUR SENSES. WHAT DO YOU FEEL, SMELL, HEAR, TASTE, AND SEE? LIST EVERYTHING YOU CAN SENSE RIGHT IN THIS MOMENT.

....

....

....

....

....

....

....

....

....

....

....

....

....

....

MEDITATION PRACTICE: Try this every day this week. Give yourself five minutes each day to sit in one place and jot down everything you sense. Do this in different environments to see how your experience stays the same or changes.

List 3

LIST THE WAYS THAT YOU TEND TO
FEEL STRESS IN YOUR BODY.

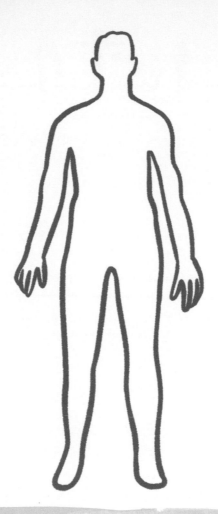

RELAXATION PRACTICE: Take a moment to check in with your whole body. Sit or lie down and close your eyes. Focus all your feeling on your feet, and breathe deeply and slowly in and out five times. Move your focus to your calves and do the same thing. Keep slowly moving through every part of your body, from your toes up to your head and then out to your fingertips, as you feel your connection to yourself. You are here. You are grounded.

List 4

CLOSE YOUR EYES. VISUALIZE A BEAUTIFUL AND
COMFORTING PLOT OF LAND. LIST OR DRAW WHAT
YOU SEE, FEEL, HEAR, AND SMELL.

BUILD A HOUSE THAT FEELS SAFE AND INVITING
ON YOUR LAND. LIST OR DRAW WHAT IT LOOKS LIKE
ON THE EXTERIOR AND ON THE INSIDE.

RELAXATION PRACTICE: The next time you
feel stressed, close your eyes and return to this
comforting space. Cultivate visiting this safe space
in your mind as a routine that is accessible to
you, no matter where you may be physically. You
have the capacity to become your own greatest
resource; comfort always exists within you.

List 5

LIST THE THOUGHTS THAT FILL YOUR MIND WHEN
YOU EXPERIENCE STRESS, WORRY, AND FEAR.

....

....

....

....

....

....

....

....

....

....

....

RELEASING EXERCISE: Once you've written down your list, tear or cut out the page it's on, or rewrite the list on a separate piece of paper, and find a safe place to light it on fire! Throw it into the flames and watch your fears disintegrate. The next time you feel stressed, worried, or scared, recall the feeling of watching your negative thoughts go up in flames. Feel free to do this exercise as often as you like.

List 6

LIST THE SONGS THAT FEEL LIKE COMFORT,
PEACE, CALM, AND REST.

....

....

....

....

....

....

....

....

....

....

....

CREATE + EXPRESS: Use this list to build your ultimate rest playlist, and fill your mind with peaceful and positive musical narratives.

List 7

SET A TIMER FOR TEN MINUTES AND LIST EVERYTHING THAT IS STRESSING YOU OUT RIGHT NOW. WHEN THE TEN MINUTES ARE UP, BE DONE THINKING ABOUT THESE THINGS.

....
....
....
....
....
....
....
....
....
....
....
....
....
....

....

....

....

....

....

....

....

....

....

BOUNDARY SETTING: Assign yourself a ten-minute window of time each day this week when you are allowed to think about all the hard things in your life. When you give yourself a set time to feel and consider the heaviness around you, you are setting healthy boundaries. Stress is a normal part of being human; it's a trigger in our body telling us, "Hey! Here's something that is not sustainable." That innate part of ourselves is a lot easier to manage if we practice setting internal limits on how long we allow ourselves to think about stressful things, and external limits on how long we allow stressful situations to continue in our lives.

Let everything
happen to you:
beauty and terror.

Just keep going.
No feeling is final.

—RAINER MARIA RILKE

List 8

LIST THE PEOPLE YOU DON'T KNOW IN REAL LIFE WHOM
YOU FIND SOOTHING. THIS COULD INCLUDE AUTHORS,
CELEBRITIES, OR PEOPLE YOU FOLLOW ON SOCIAL MEDIA.

··

··

··

··

··

··

··

··

··

··

··

DATA-GATHERING EXERCISE: Reach out to the people on this list (hey, you might be surprised to hear back!) and gather data on what brings them peace and calm. If reaching out is too scary, scan their social media for inspiring and soothing quotes and images. Add the recommendations you like to your tool kit on page 150.

List 9

LIST THE WAYS YOU CURRENTLY TRY
TO MANAGE YOUR STRESS.

....

....

....

....

....

....

....

....

....

....

....

....

CREATE + EXPRESS: What on your list is working? Circle the things that seem to be making a difference and add those coping mechanisms to your tool kit on page 150. Is there anything you are doing to try to manage your stress that doesn't seem to be helping, or is even backfiring? If so, perhaps finding someone to guide you in anxiety management might help. (See How to Find a Therapist on page 158.)

List 10

LIST THE SONGS THAT MAKE
YOU WANT TO MOVE!

··

··

··

··

··

··

··

··

CREATE + EXPRESS: Use this list to build your active-energy playlist. It may seem counterintuitive to dance or shake out your body when your mind feels overwhelmed, but if your brain is already buzzing and active, you can transform that into physical energy. Visualize the stress as hanging out in a part of your body, and *get it out*. Shake, dance, move, bounce around, and release. Make it silly.

List 11

LIST THE FEELINGS AND THOUGHTS THAT
COME UP WHEN YOU ARE AVOIDING
SOMETHING OR PROCRASTINATING.

....

....

....

....

....

....

....

....

....

CLARIFYING EXERCISE: Do you prefer to break up projects into smaller tasks that you can do day by day? Or do you prefer to have one big chunk of time to power through the whole thing? Either way is okay! Some people are able to chip away at big projects, whereas others are sprinters, which means that they get their best work done, get the most inspiration, and feel the most satisfied when they work fast and hard. The next time you feel anxiety rising from putting something off, instead remember how you work best, and assign yourself a day (or a series of days) and a place to work on that thing.

I prefer a ☐ slow-and-steady pace.
☐ fast-and-efficient pace.

List 12

LIST ALL THE THINGS YOU WOULD LIKE TO BE
ABLE TO DO WITH MORE EASE AND LIGHTNESS,
AND LESS WORRY, ANXIETY, OR FEAR.

....

....

....

....

....

....

....

....

....

....

....

....

....

....

....

....

....

....

....

....

....

....

BALANCE EXERCISE: These are your goals as you move through the rest of this journal. For now, circle one thing to focus on for the next two months. (It takes thirty days to break a habit, and thirty more days to establish a new healthy pattern.) What is one little thing you can practice doing to make that item on your list feel a little bit lighter, easier, and calmer? Write it down.

One little way I can bring lightness and calm to my life:

....

Look Back

We cannot choose our external circumstances, but we can always choose how we respond to them.

—EPICTETUS

———————————

One of the most transformative things ever said to me was, "I hear you saying everything you *don't* want to be but nothing you *do* want to be." My very first therapist nailed it, and a lightbulb went on in my mind.

Often, we get so caught up in the narratives happening around us that we can lose track of what is true to our deepest, most authentic selves. Living in reaction to people, situations, and our environment feels very different from focusing first on how *you* want to engage with them. The things that have happened *to* you are real things, with real impact. You can't control those things, and that is okay. But you and only you are the one who can decide how you use those experiences to better your life and the lives of those around you moving forward.

———————————

YOU ARE RESILIENT.

List 13

LIST THE LABELS AND EXPECTATIONS THAT
HAVE BEEN PLACED ON YOU BY FAMILY,
FRIENDS, COLLEAGUES, AND OTHERS.

....

....

....

....

....

....

....

....

....

....

RELEASING EXERCISE: Look through these labels and expectations and consider this: If someone else had never applied them to you, would you have chosen them for yourself? Cross out the labels and expectations that don't feel authentic to who you are. You are the only person who can truly define who you are and how it is best for you to live.

List 14

LIST THE OBJECTS, PEOPLE, AND PLACES
FROM YOUR CHILDHOOD THAT BROUGHT YOU
COMFORT AND HAPPINESS.

....
....
....
....
....
....
....
....
....
....
....
....
....
....
....

CREATING A POSITIVE REMINDER: Choose an object in your home that you would like to cultivate as a source of calm and comfort. Every time you look at it this week, take a moment to touch it and say the word "calm" to yourself. Draw this object, along with an object from your childhood that brought you comfort, in your tool kit on page 150.

List 15

LIST THE BELIEFS AND VALUES THAT
INFLUENCE YOUR DECISION-MAKING.

....

....

....

....

....

....

....

....

....

....

RELEASING EXERCISE: Reflect on some of the big and little decisions you have made in the last week. Do those decisions align with the things you just listed about your personal values? Guess what—no one lives by the ideals they hold themselves to 100 percent of the time, and that is okay! It does not make you a bad person; it makes you human, beautifully flawed and worthy of self-acceptance, compassion, and understanding. Your imperfection is what makes you human, not a robot, so perhaps you can ease up a little on how much you expect of yourself. You're doing a great job.

List 16

LIST THE THINGS YOU ARE MOST
PROUD OF OVERCOMING.

. . . .

. . . .

. . . .

. . . .

. . . .

. . . .

. . . .

. . . .

. . . .

. . . .

. . . .

. . . .

. . . .

AFFIRMATION EXERCISE: Underline the things on this list that you feel you had to push through stress and anxiety to overcome. Is there anything you are currently facing that reminds you of things you have already overcome? Think of your past experiences as practice for the present and future. You've done the work before, and you can do it again.

List 17

LIST THE TIMES YOU HAVE BENEFITED FROM SLOWING
DOWN, PULLING BACK, OR SAYING NO.

....

....

....

....

....

....

....

....

....

....

....

....

....

....

....

....

....

....

....

....

....

....

....

....

RELAXATION EXERCISE: Try a breathing exercise, called the calming response, to relieve your anxious energy. Breathe in for a count of four. Pause and gently hold your breath for a count of four. Breathe out for a count of four. Pause for a count of four. Repeat this cycle as many times as it feels soothing to you. When we feel panicked and our stress levels rise, we often find ourselves in fight-or-flight mode, a.k.a. in an emergency response. To counter that trigger to quickly react, try the calming response, which will help bring peace to your nervous system.

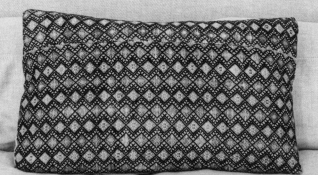

List 18

LIST THE FOODS AND DRINKS THAT SOOTHE YOU.

....

....

....

....

....

....

....

....

....

....

....

....

....

....

....

....

....

....

....

....

....

....

....

....

....

....

RELAXATION EXERCISE: Make or buy yourself a meal that is comforting to you. Put your phone away and allow yourself the time and space to just sit and eat your food, and to savor the experience with all of your senses. When your mind starts to wander, gently bring your attention back to the flavors and sensations. Add your favorite comfort foods to your tool kit on page 150.

List 19

LIST ALL THE ACTIVITIES YOU HAVE DONE
OVER THE COURSE OF YOUR LIFE THAT
BROUGHT YOU STRESS RELIEF OR CALM.

....

....

....

....

....

....

....

....

....

....

REFLECT + RELEASE: Bring one of these activities back into your life! Go down your list and choose the activity that sounds the most fun and approachable, and then challenge yourself to do it at least once by the end of the week.

Fear makes the past repeat itself. Hope uses the past as a teaching mechanism to create a different future.

—BUNNY MICHAEL

List 20

LIST THE WAYS YOU ARE DIFFERENT NOW THAN
YOU WERE IN THE PAST.

....

....

....

....

....

....

....

....

....

....

....

....

....

....

....

....

....

....

....

....

....

....

....

....

....

....

....

....

MOTIVATION PRACTICE: If you have the capacity to be different today than you were in the past, then you have the capacity to make changes in the present that will impact you for the better in the future. What is one little way you can make tomorrow 1 percent better than today? Answer this question every night before bed for a week. If you like it, feel free to continue!

List 21

LIST THE THINGS ABOUT YOURSELF THAT YOU FEEL
SHY OR SCARED ABOUT EXPRESSING.

....

....

....

....

....

....

....

....

....

....

....

....

....

··

··

··

··

··

··

··

··

··

RELEASING EXERCISE: It's important to feel like you get to be your authentic self at least some of the time, and you deserve the space to express whatever is inside of you. The longer you keep it in, the more potential it has to become something powerful and negative. And the quicker you can get it out of your body physically—by writing it down and allowing it to exist—the lighter you will feel. If you're uncomfortable seeing your most private thoughts on paper, that's okay! Feel free to tear out the page you've written on, or scribble out your words, if you need to in order to feel safe. The important thing is to get your thoughts out.

List 22

LIST THE BOOK AND MOVIE CHARACTERS YOU ADMIRE WHO HAVE PERSEVERED THROUGH CHALLENGES TO GET TO A BETTER SPACE—PHYSICALLY, MENTALLY, OR EMOTIONALLY.

CLARIFYING EXERCISE: How did each of these characters prevail and get to a better state of being? Write down the qualities that helped each of them persevere next to their names, and underline the qualities you see in yourself.

List 23

LIST ALL THE PEOPLE IN YOUR LIFE THAT YOU HAVE FELT
COMFORTABLE TALKING TO AND FELT HEARD BY.

....

....

....

....

....

....

....

....

....

....

....

....

....

....

....

....

....

....

....

....

....

REFLECTION EXERCISE: Of those people, who are you still close with? Add their names and contact info to your tool kit on page 150, so that you'll know who you can call when you need someone to talk to. If none of the people you listed are still in your life, there are many other resources waiting to support you. Try visiting 7Cups.com to chat with a trained volunteer listener for free emotional support. Or consider seeing a therapist to have a professional, caring, and unbiased ear. (See How to Find a Therapist on page 158.)

List 24

LIST THE FAILURES THAT HAVE LED TO EVENTUAL
SUCCESS AND ACCOMPLISHMENT FOR YOU.

....

....

....

....

....

....

....

....

....

....

....

PERSPECTIVE CHANGE: Failures aren't really failures; they're just stepping stones to success. A failure is merely an experiment with an outcome that gives you data for how you could do things differently for a better result. What is one thing you have done recently that didn't work out the first time but that you want to improve? Write it down and plan to try it again.

....

....

List 25

LIST ALL THE COMPANIONS, BE THEY HUMAN OR
ANIMAL, FROM YOUR PAST THAT HAVE HAD A
CALMING INFLUENCE ON YOUR LIFE.

List 26

LIST THE MOVIES AND TV SHOWS
THAT BRING YOU CALM.

....

....

....

....

....

....

....

....

....

....

RELAXATION PRACTICE: Watch one of your favorite calming movies or TV shows tonight! Bonus points if you also make yourself a drink that soothes you and cozy up in a space that brings you calm. Add your top five most calming movies and shows to your tool kit on page 150.

List 27

IMAGINE YOURSELF AT FOURTEEN. LIST THE WAYS YOU
WOULD HAVE DESCRIBED YOURSELF *AT THE TIME*.

NOW, DESCRIBE YOURSELF AT FOURTEEN WITH ALL THE
WISDOM AND EMPATHY OF YOUR CURRENT AGE.

....

....

....

....

....

....

....

....

....

....

....

....

....

....

CLARIFYING EXERCISE: Sometimes wisdom comes
with age, and sometimes wisdom lives in youth, and
every version of you deserves love and acceptance.
Underline the positive qualities you held in the past
that you would like to celebrate in the present.

Move Forward

In three words I can sum up everything
I've learned about life: it goes on.

—ROBERT FROST

———

Our past is merely evidence of our existence. And for many of us, simply existing is a feat in itself. It is fair to want your life to be different—maybe you're not satisfied with what has already happened or what is happening in this moment. But that doesn't mean the life you have known thus far has to entirely end to start anew.

You are allowed to pivot, to take one little step in a new direction that will lead you, one step at a time, from the negative of the past into the positive of a better future. So take those first steps in a new direction with you as your own guide. You have the capacity to initiate and create change for yourself on your own terms.

———

YOU ARE COURAGEOUS.

List 28

LIST THE ROUTINES IN YOUR DAY, WEEK, OR
MONTH THAT BRING YOU EASE OF MIND.

....

....

....

....

....

....

....

....

....

....

....

....

....

MINDFULNESS EXERCISE: In a sense, routines are
an opportunity for mindfulness and an opportunity
for your mind to rest in the moment. As you flow
through your routines this week, allow yourself
to be present in your tasks instead of constantly
planning the next thing. When you finish a routine,
take a moment to pause, breathe, and experience
gratitude before moving on.

List 29

LIST THE THINGS OUTSIDE OF ROUTINES
THAT BRING YOU JOY.

....

....

....

....

....

....

....

....

....

....

....

....

POSITIVE COMPARTMENTALIZATION: Add five of these things to your calendar in the upcoming weeks and months. Being able to look forward to something in the future can make the stress of the present feel a little more manageable.

List 30

LIST THE PEOPLE YOU THINK OF AS
YOUR CHOSEN FAMILY.

....

....

....

....

....

....

....

....

....

....

....

....

....

CLARIFYING EXERCISE: Chosen family members are individuals who deliberately choose one another to play significant roles in each other's lives, defined by what they decide family looks like to them, rather than what society says family should look like. Choose one or two words or phrases for each person in your chosen family that explain why they feel like family to you, and write those next to their names.

List 31

LIST THE THINGS YOU CAN TOUCH THAT
ARE PHYSICALLY CALMING TO YOU.

List 32

LIST THE ACTIVITIES YOU'D IDEALLY
LIKE TO BE SPENDING YOUR TIME ON.

BOUNDARY SETTING: Do you wish you had a little more time to invest in activities and experiences offscreen? If so, try downloading an app (like Moment, ZenScreen, or Flipd) that will track how much time you spend on your phone/computer/tablet and the websites and apps you engage with every day. Record your findings here. Then add your own philosophy of how to use technology mindfully to your tool kit on page 150.

When we deny the story, it defines us. When we own the story, we can write a brave new ending.

—BRENÉ BROWN

List 33

LIST THE NEGATIVE NARRATIVES YOU REPEAT
TO YOURSELF IN YOUR MIND.

....

....

....

....

....

....

....

....

....

....

....

....

....

....

....

....

....

....

....

....

....

AFFIRMATION EXERCISE: Think of someone you respect and love—like a child, friend, or family member. How would you feel if you knew they were saying these sorts of negative things to themselves? Cross out all the things that you wouldn't want someone you love thinking about themselves. You don't deserve to think those things of yourself either. You are worthy of being accepted and respected by yourself just as you accept and respect your loved ones.

List 34

LIST THE INDOOR SPACES WHERE YOU HAVE FELT THE
MOST COMFORTABLE OVER THE COURSE OF YOUR
LIFE—AT HOME, AT WORK, OR ELSEWHERE.

....

....

....

....

....

....

....

....

....

....

....

....

....

....

....

....

....

....

....

....

....

....

....

....

....

....

MOOD-BOOSTING EXERCISE: Add your top five indoor spaces and the positive feelings you associate with each setting to your tool kit on page 150. Sometimes it takes a shift in environment to shift our mood!

List 35

LIST THE OUTDOOR PLACES THAT MAKE
YOU FEEL AT PEACE.

....

....

....

....

....

....

....

....

....

....

....

....

....

....

....

....

....

....

....

....

....

....

....

....

....

....

GROUNDING EXERCISE: Add your top five outdoor places and the positive feelings you associate with each setting to your tool kit on page 150.

List 36

LIST THE THINGS YOU HAVE BEEN TOLD *NOT* TO DO.

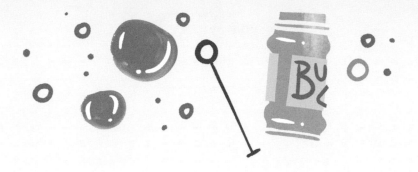

....

....

....

....

....

....

....

....

AFFIRMATION EXERCISE: Look at your list and ask yourself, "Who is the true person stopping me from doing these things?" It's not the person who told you no; only *you* are the final decision maker in control of your actions and thoughts. Review your list of your beliefs and values, List 15, and circle any of the things in this list you've been told not to do that align with your values—and that you actually might want to do. Make a plan to do one thing on your list that feels safe and positive to you. Remember, you get to live your life by your own standards.

List 37

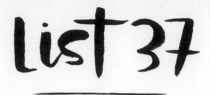

LIST THE SKILLS AND QUALITIES YOU HAVE RIGHT NOW
THAT MAKE YOU FEEL PREPARED TO HANDLE THE
FUTURE, WHATEVER MAY COME.

....

....

....

....

....

....

....

....

....

....

....

....

....

AFFIRMATION EXERCISE: Look at how capable you are! How many of these skills and qualities did you learn or develop because of having to adapt to a past difficult experience? Underline these as a reminder to yourself that even in hard times, you have prevailed, and you've created tools to help yourself because of it.

List 38

LIST EVERYTHING YOU THOUGHT ABOUT
WHEN YOU WOKE UP TODAY.

TONIGHT, LIST EVERYTHING YOU THINK ABOUT BEFORE GOING TO BED.

....

....

....

....

....

....

....

....

....

....

....

RELEASING EXERCISE: Is there a certain time of day when you experience more anxious thoughts than other times? For the week ahead, keep a notepad by your bed and write down any anxious thoughts you have as they come to you—both immediately after you wake up and just before you fall asleep. If you have tasks that are nagging at you, let the paper hold your reminder to take care of it later, rather than letting it continuously swirl in your mind. You deserve rest.

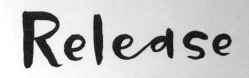

Release

When I let go of what I am, I become what I might be.
When I let go of what I have, I receive what I need.

—LAO TZU

We've all heard the phrase "Live for today." But how do we actually actively engage with today without worrying about tomorrow or letting our mind ruminate endlessly on the past? It takes acceptance—of who you are right now and where you are right now. Days themselves are not tasks meant to be accomplished, though we may have tasks we want to get done within each day. The tasks and accomplishments themselves are not what bring value to your day or who you are. Some days are just for existing peacefully, for passing through each encounter in your day as it comes.

It might sound like the opposite of what you've heard all your life, but what if you didn't strive to do your best every day? What if you saved your best for just very special situations? Not every meal you prepare, every time you clean your house, or every project you do at work needs to be amazing. At first, it might feel uncomfortable not trying your hardest all the time, but done is often better than perfect. And there is freedom to be found in just completing something, even if it's not "the best."

Just like your body needs rest to feel replenished, your heart and mind need rest too, so that you can thrive. The things that deserve your deepest thoughts and most loving heart will benefit from the time you have allowed yourself to simply exist while you move through your life. You already have everything you need, within yourself, to feel free from the pressures of the world around you.

YOU ARE FREE.

List 39

LIST YOUR HAPPY DISTRACTIONS.

RELAXATION EXERCISE: These are the things that take your mind off the hard stuff and give your brain a break. It's healthy to give your mind and heart time to rest and not think or feel sometimes. Why do you think reality TV is so popular? Occasional zone-outs are good! Indulge in one of your happy distractions today, and add a few favorites to your tool kit on page 150.

List 40

LIST THE THINGS YOU WOULD SAY TO OTHER
PEOPLE IF YOU HAD THE COURAGE.

....

....

....

....

....

....

....

....

....

RELEASING EXERCISE: How do you feel after getting these thoughts and feelings onto the page? For now, expressing yourself by writing is a great start. Come back to this page in four or five days and reread what you wrote. Do you still feel the same way? If so, go through your list and decide if you can find a way to let some of these things go or make a plan to have some of these conversations.

List 41

LIST THE THINGS YOU ARE LOOKING FORWARD
TO REPEATING IN YOUR LIFE.

....

....

....

....

....

....

....

....

....

....

....

....

....

....

....

....

....

....

....

....

....

....

....

....

....

....

POSITIVE REPETITION: So often, we focus on what we *don't* want to repeat from the past. What if we directed our attention to focusing on what we *do* want to repeat? This week, make a plan to re-create a positive experience, like wearing an outfit you feel great in or repeating an activity you loved doing with a friend—be it something from a few weeks ago or a few years ago. Notice the comforting vibes that it brings back to you.

List 42

LIST OUT THE DETAILS OF THE WORST-CASE SCENARIO FOR
SOMETHING YOU ARE STRESSED ABOUT RIGHT NOW.

RELEASING EXERCISE: Sometimes, naming the thing you are afraid of, and then assessing how likely it is to actually happen, can remove some of its power and bring that power back into your hands. After describing your worst-case scenario, write out the best possible scenario in the lines below, and then a middle ground between worst and best. There are always more potential outcomes than the worst option.

BEST POSSIBLE SCENARIO:

....

....

....

....

....

....

MIDDLE GROUND:

....

....

....

....

....

....

List 43

LIST THE THINGS IN YOUR LIFE THAT YOU
WOULD LIKE TO SIMPLIFY.

....

....

....

....

....

....

....

....

....

....

....

....

....

....
....
....
....
....
....
....
....
....

CLARIFYING EXERCISE: Of the things you listed, underline the ones that are physical (like decluttering your shoe collection) and start there. Choose one of these things to work on simplifying this week, and then come back to this list as you have time to keep going. You'll be amazed at how making even a bit of physical space creates mental space as well!

List 44

LIST THE THINGS THAT YOU WOULD LIKE TO HAVE
MORE OF OR DO MORE OF IN YOUR LIFE.

....

....

....

....

....

....

....

....

....

....

....

....

CLARIFYING EXERCISE: We all have a finite amount of time, energy, space, and money. Go through the list you just made and label what you would need more of to make each thing happen: Is it time, energy, space, or money? Now, think about which of these four things would be easiest for you to create more of, and circle it below.

TIME   ENERGY

SPACE   MONEY

List 45

LIST THE SITUATIONS IN WHICH YOUR
IMAGINATION SERVES YOU WELL.

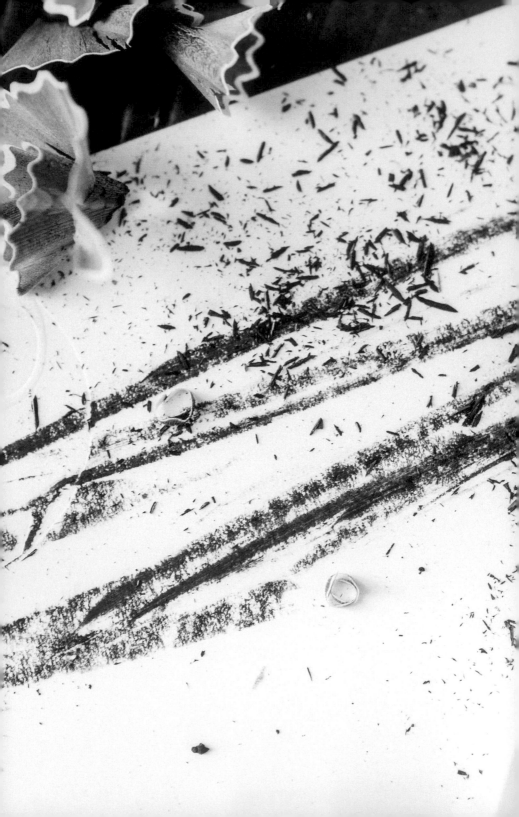

You are an amazing and emotional person who feels feelings. This can be annoying sometimes but it's also your secret power. Keep being human.

—ADAM J. KURTZ

List 46

LIST THE TIMES WHEN DAYDREAMING TAKES OR HAS
TAKEN AWAY FROM LIVING IN THE PRESENT.

....

....

....

....

....

....

....

....

BOUNDARY SETTING: It's a lot easier to live in a world of dreams than to live in the present. But the longer you spend living in your dreams, the less you will get to actually *live* your life, which is ticking by each day. Tomorrow evening, plan to give yourself a solid thirty minutes to just dream. Take action to get what you need to get done earlier during the day, knowing that you can look forward to dreaming and imagining when the sun goes down.

List 47

LIST THE NICE THINGS YOU DO FOR OTHERS.

....

....

....

....

....

....

....

....

....

....

REFRAMING PRACTICE: Being nice and being kind are not the same thing. While something might seem like the nice thing to do for someone in the moment, perhaps a kinder thing would be to *not* do that thing, but instead to challenge and help that person learn to do it for themselves. As the saying goes, "Give a man a fish and you feed him for a day; teach a man to fish and you feed him for a lifetime." Circle one thing on your list of nice things that you want to stop doing for someone else, and come up with a plan to help them do it for themselves.

List 48

LIST THE QUOTES THAT INSPIRE CALM FOR YOU.

....

....

....

....

....

....

....

....

....

....

....

....

....

....

....

....

....

....

....

....

....

....

....

CREATE + EXPRESS: Choose one of these quotes and make a piece of art inspired by the words, or print out the quote, frame it, and hang it on your wall as a daily reminder of the calm you seek to cultivate.

List 49

LIST THE PHYSICAL ACTIVITIES YOU
ACTUALLY ENJOY DOING.

....

....

....

....

....

....

....

....

....

....

RELEASING EXERCISE: So often, society pressures us to get physical for the sole purpose of changing our body to become more attractive to others. But your body is yours, not anyone else's. You deserve to be able to move your body for the simple joy of movement—because it feels good. This week, plan to do something active just for fun. Release expectations and the desire for results, and just act on your desire to move. Afterwards, add a physical activity or two from your list above to your tool kit on page 150.

List 50

LIST SOME THINGS THAT BRING
PURPOSE TO YOUR LIFE.

....

....

....

....

....

....

....

....

....

....

....

....

....

....

....

....

....

....

....

....

....

....

....

....

VALIDATION EXERCISE: It's okay if right now it's hard to come up with ideas of what is meaningful and why you live your life. But one thing is for sure: you exist. And there is purpose simply in that. On the lines below, write out this sentence and sign your name, acknowledging it as truth. "I exist. I am here. That is purpose enough for me."

....

....

SIGNED: ....

List 51

LIST THE WORDS YOU ASSOCIATE WITH CALM.

....

....

....

....

....

....

....

....

....

....

....

....

....

....
....
....
....
....
....
....
....
....
....

MEDITATION PRACTICE: Choose a few of these calming words and put them together as a simple mantra, like "May I feel peaceful"—or create a haiku! Try repeating your mantra in your head the next time you are feeling stressed-out. Add your mantra to your tool kit on page 150.

List 52

LIST HOW YOU FEEL TODAY IN YOUR BODY, MIND, AND
HEART. THEN LOOK BACK AT YOUR FIRST LIST. WHERE
DO YOU SEE POSITIVE CHANGE AND PROGRESS?

....

....

....

....

....

....

VALIDATION EXERCISE: Breathe and live. You are incredible. It takes a lot of courage and vulnerability to pursue loving, accepting, understanding, and caring for yourself well. And you now not only have a whole book of reflections and insights on your own experience with managing anxiety and stress, but you've also developed your own personalized tool kit, on page 150, for when you feel stress again. This book is no longer a journal; it has become a personalized reference book for a customized wellness practice, just for you. Take pride in all you have discovered within these pages and transformed within yourself. The peaceful life you want is at your fingertips, so exhale, move forward, and live it!

My Tool Kit
for Calm

THINGS TO BE AWARE OF THAT TRIGGER MY STRESS

PRACTICES THAT MAKE ME FEEL GROUNDED AND CENTERED

CALMING INSPIRATION FROM PEOPLE I ADMIRE

WAYS I CAN MANAGE STRESS THAT FEEL HELPFUL

MY FAVORITE HAPPY DISTRACTIONS

MY COMFORT OBJECTS, PAST AND PRESENT

WAYS I CAN USE TECHNOLOGY MORE MINDFULLY

PEOPLE I CAN TALK TO

MY COMFORT FOODS

MY FAVORITE CALM MOVIES AND SHOWS

MY INDOOR CALM SPACES

MY OUTDOOR CALM PLACES

MY FAVORITE PHYSICAL ACTIVITIES

MY PERSONAL CALMING MANTRA

A KIT FOR CALMING, CENTERING, AND GROUNDING

Create a calming physical kit with objects you can take with you on the go or keep in a special place! Just like having a first-aid kit for physical wounds, it can help to have a kit for emotional and psychological hurts. Get a bag or box and fill it with things that soothe: Perhaps a smooth rock that you can touch to feel grounded, or dark chocolate that you can nibble on to raise your endorphin and serotonin levels. Perhaps a written poem that you can read, or the lyrics from a song, to uplift you; lavender essential oil that you can smell to experience calm; or peppermint gum or tea, which will not only engage your taste buds but can lower inflammation as well (which is often connected to depression and anxiety). Keep your little bag or box of comfort and calm in your backpack or purse, by your nightstand, or in a drawer at work!

RESOURCES FOR CALM

Instagram

@anxiety_wellbeing

@anxietysupport.info

@bunnymichael

@thehappynewspaper

@journey_to_wellness_

@makedaisychains

@positivelypresent

@recipesforselflove

@selfcareisforeveryone

@stacieswift

Adult Books

- *The Anxiety Toolkit* by Alice Boyes, PhD

- *The Anxiety & Worry Workbook* by David A. Clark and Aaron T. Beck

- *The Autoimmune Paleo Cookbook* by Mickey Trescott

- *The Autoimmune Wellness Handbook* by Mickey Trescott

- *The Healthy Mind Toolkit* by Alice Boyes, PhD

- *It's OK to Feel Things Deeply* by Carissa Potter

Kids' Books

- *A Handful of Quiet* by Thich Nhat Hanh

- *I Can Handle It* by Laurie Wright

- *Listening to My Body* by Gabi Garcia

- *Master of Mindfulness* by Laurie Grossman

- *Sitting Still Like a Frog* by Eline Snel

Apps, Podcasts, and Websites

- *Anxiety and Depression Association of America (ADAA.org)*

- *The Anxiety Coaches Podcast (TheAnxietyCoachesPodcast.com)*

- *Calm (Calm.com)*

- *Headspace (Headspace.com)*

- *The Mighty (TheMighty.com)*

- *Oprah's SuperSoul Conversations (SuperSoul.tv)*

Hotlines

- *Crisis Text Line (text HOME to 741741)*

- *National Sexual Assault Hotline (1-800-656-4673)*

- *National Suicide Prevention Lifeline (1-800-273-8255)*

- *TrevorLifeline for LGBTQ Youth (1-866-488-7386)*

How to Find a Therapist

- The difference between a psychiatrist and a psychologist: Psychologists (a.k.a. therapists) focus extensively on treating their clients' emotional and mental suffering with talk and behavioral intervention. Psychiatrists, on the other hand, are medical professionals who spend much of their time prescribing medications for their clients and managing those medications as a course of treatment. I recommend first talking with a psychologist. Your psychologist can then recommend you to a psychiatrist if you need additional support.

- If you have insurance, your insurance provider should have a list of therapists that are within your network. Visit your provider's website or give them a call to obtain this list.

- Don't have insurance? That's okay! Go to OpenPathCollective .org to find a sliding-scale therapist in your area.

- Just need someone to talk to who feels safe? Check out one of these amazing organizations, some of which have 24/7 access to licensed counselors.

    - 7Cups.com
    - BetterHelp.com
    - Breakthrough.com
    - Talkspace.com

- You don't have to settle for the first therapist you visit! Try testing out three therapists, one session each, to see which one you vibe with best. Yeah, it's kind of like dating, but when you find a therapist who really gets you, it will make a world of difference.

- Do you have something specific you want help with? Most therapists specialize in multiple fields—like anxiety and panic disorders, substance abuse, eating disorders, marriage and family counseling, etc. Try the "Find a Therapist" feature on the Psychology Today website (PsychologyToday.com /us/therapists)—it makes it easy to search for specialties within a geographical area, and even by insurance plan. You can also search therapists by specialty in the "Find a Therapist Directory" on the website of the Anxiety and Depression Association of America: Members.ADAA.org /page/FATMain. For an international therapist directory, see InternationalTherapistDirectory.com.

- I recommend starting with cognitive behavioral therapy (CBT), the most common type of talk therapy that can help you manage challenges by changing the way you think and behave. It's often used to treat anxiety and depression as well as many other mental and physical health problems. Your cognitive behavioral therapist can refer you to other types of therapy if needed.

- Do you come from a cultural or religious background with specific needs? If so, there are therapists out there who can and will understand your unique value system, upbringing, and experiences. A great therapist will be neutral in their opinions on your background and beliefs, but it's totally okay to look for a therapist who will have a deeper understanding of where you're coming from on a cultural or religious level.

- I encourage you to work with therapists who welcome people of all races, religions, sexual orientations, gender identities and expressions, countries of origin, abilities, ethnicities, and body types. Their job is to help you explore and discover who you are and what you need to be well. And the more inclusive they are, the more opportunity there is for you to connect and heal.

MOOREA SEAL is a Seattle-based author, fashion and lifestyle retailer, and designer, as well as an avid list maker whose books have been praised on Oprah.com and other media outlets. Her passion lies in helping readers and writers discover their own resiliency through list making, positive contemplation, and self-expression. When she's not adventuring with her partner, Max, and their dog, Lemon, she can be found in her Seattle store, also named Moorea Seal, and online at **MooreaSeal.com**.

SASQUATCH BOOKS with colophon is a registered trademark of Penguin Random House LLC

25 24 23 22 21 20 19   10 9 8 7 6 5 4 3 2 1

ISBN: 978-1-63217-285-3

Sasquatch Books • 1904 Third Avenue, Suite 710
Seattle, WA 98101
SasquatchBooks.com

Editor: Hannah Elnan • Production editor: Bridget Sweet • Design: Bryce de Flamand
Illustrations: Jordan Kay • Illustrated type: Julia Manchik • Photo credits: Charity Burggraaf (cover), Chelsea Albert (endsheets), © iStock.com/KatarzynaBialasiewicz (page 2), © BONNIN-STUDIO / Stocksy United (pages 12–13), © Annie Sprat (page 24), © Kelly Knox / Stocksy United (pages 27, 32–33, 44–45), Meghan Kay Sadler (pages 56, 59, 64–65, 120, 132–133, 142), © Alina Hvostikova / Stocksy United (page 68), © Leandro Crespi / Stocksy United (page 71), ID 73567714 © Marnie Patchett | Dreamstime.com (pages 84–85), © iStock.com/passigatti (pages 98–99), © Calvin Chou (pages 112–113), © Max Nguyen (page 123), Bethanie Marie (page 145)